Introduction to

HARDNESS
OF
HEART

Andrew Wommack

Published by Andrew Wommack Ministries, Inc.

Woodland Park, CO 80863

ISBN 13 TP: 978-1-59548-787-2

For Worldwide Distribution, Printed in the USA

1 2 3 4 5 6 / 28 27 26 25

CONTENTS

Would you like to get more out of this teaching?

Scan the QR code to access this teaching in video or audio formats to help you dive even deeper as you study.

Accessing the teaching this way will help you get even more out of this booklet.

awmi.net/browse

INTRODUCTION

Years ago, not long after the Lord radically transformed my life on March 23, 1968, I started seeing things in the Bible like I'd never seen them before. Those verses had always been there, but they just began to jump out at me. One of the things I got really excited about was healing.

These days, we see numerous people healed through our ministry and even host the annual Healing is Here event at our Charis Bible College campus in Woodland Park, Colorado. But when I first got the revelation on healing, I was so steeped in religion that I had no idea if anyone had been miraculously healed since the time of the apostles!

So, when I saw in the Word of God that healing was possible, I was determined to see it work in my life. But when the first person I prayed for was actually healed, I was as surprised as anybody else. That's just the way I started out ministering. Every time I laid hands on somebody, I'd wonder, *God, is this going to work?*

Did you know that being shocked or surprised by a miracle indicates that you have a hardened heart? When the Lord moves in a person's life, and they experience something miraculous, they may think, *God, I'll never doubt you again!* But in reality, it's only a matter of time before they come into another situation and, instead of looking to God, they look to the natural for a solution.

Their previous experience with God had no lasting impact. That's an indicator of a hardened heart.

Jesus said more than once during His ministry, *"He that hath ears to hear, let him hear"* (Mark 4:9 and Luke 8:8). Every person He was speaking to had physical ears. But He wasn't talking about physical hearing. Jesus was talking about hearing with the heart.

Did you know that you have more than just your five physical senses? You also have a heart with which you can see and hear spiritual things. Faith allows born-again people to perceive things with their hearts that they couldn't otherwise get.

You may be wondering, *Where is the heart that allows me to perceive spiritual things?* It's not your physical blood pump. It is the invisible core of who you are—made up of your spirit and soul. When your spirit and soul work together, you can perceive things with your heart.

'I DON'T BELIEVE IT!'

I thought that a person with a hardened heart was someone who hated God—a person who was living in open rebellion and deliberately sinning against the Lord. I thought it was somebody who was going the other way and just didn't care.

Although a person like that does indeed have a hardened heart, the condition is typically more subtle, which is why many people don't realize it applies to them. Anybody who is cold, insensitive, unfeeling, or unyielding to God in any area of their life has a hardened heart.

If people would just be honest, there are areas of their lives where they just don't seem to be connecting with the Lord. It's easier for them to relate to the natural realm than the supernatural. It's easier to relate to living in defeat than having victory by faith.

Years ago, I was ministering in Omaha, Nebraska, and I was calling out healings through the gifts of the Holy Spirit (1 Cor. 12:4–11). I said somebody had crossed eyes and should come forward. There was a young boy, probably ten to twelve years old, and his eyes were so crossed that he had to have someone lead him by the hand. He just couldn't see very well.

When I laid hands on that boy, I put my thumbs over his eyes, and I prayed. I was believing he would be healed. And at the time, I planned to say something encouraging to him about how God's healing power was working in him and that he would eventually see perfectly, even if he didn't experience an instant change. But when I took my hands off of him, he opened his eyes, and both of them were perfect. They were straight!

Now, I hate to admit this, but when I looked at that boy and saw that his eyes had instantly straightened, I said, "I don't believe it!" And when I said that, his eyes immediately went back to being crossed. I said, "O God, I'm sorry!" I repented.

I must have prayed over that boy for another five or ten minutes, but I never did see his eyes straighten again. I still believe the power of God hit him in that meeting, and hopefully, his eyes are straight today.

There I was, ministering the Word of God, praying for people, and believing for healing. But I just assumed he was going to be healed gradually, over a period of time. The way I responded when I saw the healing happen instantly and supernaturally revealed the hardness of my heart.

NATURAL VS. SUPERNATURAL

Many people pray for healing, yet they also look to doctors to manage their condition over time through medicine or procedures. I'm not condemning anyone for believing that way.

I'm not against doctors; I even have a doctor on my board of directors. I often say that if it weren't for doctors, most Christians would be dead! That's because the typical person is more tapped into the natural way of receiving healing than the supernatural. So much so that if someone were healed instantly and supernaturally, many people—Christians included—would say, "I can't believe it!" And I think that's the reason why most don't see more supernatural things in their lives.

Years ago, T.L. Osborn had a powerful healing ministry. He was a contemporary of ministers like Oral Roberts and Kenneth E. Hagin. But he was probably more well-known overseas than at home in the United States. He said that he could hardly get through a sermon in a foreign country without being interrupted by healings and miracles breaking out. But T.L. also said that when he ministered in America, he was almost never interrupted because the supernatural didn't manifest in his meetings in the same way.

Is that because there was more sickness in places like Africa and Asia? No. I believe it's because people in the West are more likely to turn to a doctor or medicine *first*. Again, if you use those things, I'm not condemning you. But if you're more inclined to turn to a pill than the "Gods-pill (gospel)," you are less likely to seek the supernatural healing power of God.

It used to be that I would rely on my own faith to see someone else healed. If I had to, I would minister until I saw results. I was just determined. That's how John G. Lake trained his "healing technicians" in the early twentieth century. He'd send them out and tell them not to come back until they saw healing manifest in a person. One of his ministers spent three weeks with a person before they saw them healed!

In recent years, though, I've changed my approach. I just put it out there for people to be healed and leave it up to them to receive it. That places the responsibility on the other person to reach out and take their healing by faith, which is determined by the sensitivity of their heart.

A person with a hardened heart is just someone who is more dominated by the natural realm than the supernatural. And I believe that to some degree, every single one of us has a hardened heart.

USE YOUR FAITH

And he saw them toiling in rowing; for the wind was contrary unto them: and about the fourth watch of the night he cometh unto them, walking upon the sea, and would have passed by them.

Mark 6:48

Years ago, I was on an airplane, flying across the Great Lakes, and I was reading my Bible where Jesus fed the five thousand men (Mark 6:33–44), along with women and children. Jesus took five loaves and two fishes, and they were multiplied to feed thousands of people.

The Lord took that little bit of food, blessed it, broke it, and gave it to His disciples. And then, they went and fed the people until they were absolutely full. They took up the fragments that were left over, and there was more food afterward than there was before they started. Now that's miraculous!

When I was reading this passage about feeding the multitudes, I was so into the story that I was just overwhelmed. I was thinking about what a great miracle it was. I imagined what it would've been like to be there, experience those things, see all of the people fed, and watch how they responded.

Then I came down to where it says, "*And straightway* [Jesus] *constrained his disciples to get into the ship, and to go to the other side*" (Mark 6:45). After the feeding of the multitude, Jesus told the disciples to get in a boat and go to the other side of the Sea of Galilee. Meanwhile, Jesus went to a mountain to pray. The Scripture says the disciples were crossing the Sea of Galilee in a storm and rowing against the wind in the "*fourth watch of the night*" (Mark 6:48), which would have been between 3 a.m. and 6 a.m. Here they were, struggling against the storm, and Jesus came toward them "*walking upon the sea, and would have passed by them*" (Mark 6:48).

The storm and the sea were about to kill these disciples. The boat was full of water, and it looked like they were going to sink. And here came Jesus, just walking on top of it. That just illustrates the power, authority, and command that Jesus had over the elements of nature as God manifest in the flesh (1 Tim. 3:16).

The thing that was about to kill those disciples was no big deal to Jesus. And it looked like He would have just passed them by. In other words, He didn't run out there, waving His hands and saying, "Hold on, guys! I'm coming!" But Jesus wasn't out there just to take a stroll on the water either. He came specifically to minister to His disciples because they were in trouble. But He didn't save them without their cooperation. He was looking for a response.

As a matter of fact, if you read this same story in Matthew 14:22–33, they thought Jesus was a ghost and they cried out for fear. In response, He said, "*Be not afraid*" (Matthew 14:27). Now, if He really wanted them not to fear, why didn't He just calm the sea in the first place? It's because God moves through faith.

'SORE AMAZED'

And [Jesus] *went up unto them into the ship; and the wind ceased: and they were sore amazed in themselves beyond measure, and wondered. For they considered not* the miracle *of the loaves: for their heart was hardened.*

Mark 6:51–52

As I mentioned earlier, I was riding in a plane over the Great Lakes when I read this. And I found myself just like the disciples—"*sore amazed*" at these miracles.

I remember laying my Bible on my lap and looking out the window. There was a solid layer of clouds below us. In my imagination, I saw Jesus walking on top of those clouds and sitting on the wing of the plane. It wouldn't have been any more miraculous for Him to do that than for Him to walk on the water! As I considered this, I was just awestruck!

I was thinking, *God, this is awesome! I'm really being impacted by these verses!* And then, I read Mark 6:52, which starts with the word, "*For.*" That's a conjunction linking two thoughts together, making verse 52 a commentary on the previous verse.

All of a sudden, I saw the reason why I was "*sore amazed ... beyond measure*" by Jesus feeding the 5,000 (Mark 6:34–44), walking on the water and stilling the storm (Mark 6:45–51), and translating the boat to the other side of the sea (John 6:21). I had a hardened heart. For the first time, I understood that being shocked, amazed, or surprised at a miracle is an indication of a hard heart.

It was like the Lord slapped me in the face with this truth. It just arrested me, and I began seeking the Lord about these things over the next few years. I needed to make my heart more sensitive to God, and I was committed to putting in the time and effort to get a solid revelation.

Carrie Pickett, one of the vice presidents of our ministry, along with her husband Mike, likes to say that I "marinate" things. That means when I believe the Lord has shown me something, I take some time to meditate and pray on it. I don't just go out there and share something immediately. It's not unusual for me to meditate on a passage of scripture for years until it gets deep inside me.

That's one of the reasons I don't have to remove recordings from my website. If I get more revelation on a topic, I may add to it. But, in general, I've been teaching the same things for decades because I don't teach something until it gets well established in my heart. That's why people often say, "Andrew's just the same, all of the time."

I knew a minister who told his church that he got a new revelation on something, so they should disregard anything he previously taught on the subject. But within a week, he went back to those same people and told them to forget all about the new revelation. He was going back to what he had taught before. Now, I'm not condemning him for doing that, but that's just not how I work.

From this experience, I began to realize that a hardened heart is much more than just a rebellious attitude towards God. A person who relates more to the physical world and the way things work in the natural than they relate to the supernatural way things work in God's kingdom is a person with a hardened heart.

Jesus miraculously multiplied food a second time to feed four thousand men in Mark 8. Afterward, He warned the disciples about being ware of the Pharisees' doctrine, which He referred to as leaven, but they thought He was referring to them not having enough bread. They totally missed His point. In His explanation to them, he gave some of the characteristics of a hardened heart.

SPIRITUAL PERCEPTION

And when Jesus knew it, he saith unto them, Why reason ye, because ye have no bread? perceive ye not yet, neither understand? have ye your heart yet hardened?

Mark 8:17

One of the characteristics of a hardened heart is not having spiritual perception. This applies to many people who relate more to the physical, natural realm instead of the spiritual, supernatural realm. These people may be accomplished in the natural realm. But when it comes to spiritual things and the supernatural, they are not as adept.

For example, years ago, we hired a manager for our ministry who had formerly been the president of a bank. On paper, it seemed like his experience would make him a good fit for us. But it didn't turn out that way. At the time, our income fluctuated month to month. It would be way down during some months and way up in others. My partners would sometimes give and sometimes not give.

This guy was used to running a bank. He was used to consistent revenue coming in, and here we were, not knowing how much money would come in from one month to the next. It's better now, but at the time, it was all over the place. And this guy just panicked! In the bank, if the people didn't make their loan payments, he would foreclose on them or turn them over to a collection agency. We don't do that.

He came to me one month and said, "Do you realize that we've got more expenses this month than income?" And I said, "Yes, I understand that." The next month, he came to me again and said, "We still have more expenses than we've got income." And I said, "I hear you."

Then, the month after that, this man came to me and said, "You aren't listening! This is the third month in a row that our income is less than our expenses!" He was panicking and said, "You've got to do something!" But because of experiences I'd had throughout my life and ministry, I knew it just wasn't that big of a deal. I had a different perspective. My spiritual perception was sensitive to what God had done in the past. I relied on that knowledge more than what the natural realm was telling me.

One of those experiences that gave me that confidence happened during a board meeting at my house. Our income was very small, probably less than five hundred thousand dollars a year. And on paper, we were broke. Our board said, "You are bankrupt. We're going to close the ministry down."

I didn't believe it was what God wanted, but I didn't really have much of an argument to make. So, I said, "Well, let's pray." And while we were praying, the phone rang. On the other end was my mother, who was opening the mail for our ministry. She said, "We just got a $60,000 check!" It was an offering from a church that I'd never been to before or since. And it covered all of our shortfall!

That banker had never seen money come in by faith before. As one of my current financial controllers told me just last week, "ledgers don't operate by faith." I understood that and told him I appreciated him doing what he had to do to keep the books correctly. But I went on to say, "…*whatsoever is not of faith is sin*" (Rom. 14:23). I walk by faith (2 Cor. 5:7).

In Mark 8:18, Jesus said another characteristic of a hardened heart was not being able to remember. This is a big one.

I have people tell me often that I must have a photographic memory because I can quote so many scriptures. In the next breath, they tell me they just can't remember scriptures. Yet they can remember the major league batting averages of hundreds of baseball players, or the stats on all the football players and teams. They remember movies, actors, and songs, but I don't remember those things.

It's not a matter of a photographic memory but focus. I have watched some games, seen some movies, and listened to some songs, but that's not where my heart is. The reason others can remember those things and not remember scripture is that they care more about those things than they do the Word of God. I care more about God's Word than I do those other things. My heart has become sensitive to God's Word because of my commitment to it.

'THEY CONSIDERED NOT'

For they considered not the miracle *of the loaves: for their heart was hardened.*

Mark 6:52

We should always be blessed by the miraculous power of God, but not surprised or shocked. If we're shocked, it means we've been meditating on the things of the world more than the things of God. Do you think, when Jesus saw the bread and fish multiply and feed the multitude, that He was amazed or shocked? No way! He expected it. He would have been shocked if it hadn't happened.

If we are shocked by the miraculous, it's an indication of a hardened heart. When we keep our minds on the things of God, we remain in a state of faith and expectation—all things are possible (Matt. 19:26, Mark 9:23, and 10:27).

What determines the hardness or sensitivity of our hearts?

What we consider, or focus on, our hearts become sensitive to. The word "consider" means "to study, ponder, deliberate, examine, focus on, or meditate on."[1] What we fail to consider, our hearts become hardened to (Ex. 7:23). This is just the way the Lord made us. We have to cooperate with this law of God and focus on His truths to keep our hearts sensitive and receptive.

The disciples in the boat hadn't been doing anything we consider sinful. They had simply been occupied with their natural circumstances while trying to save their lives. Even today, preoccupation with everyday life will harden our hearts to the Lord. We have to make a deliberate effort to look beyond our daily responsibilities and keep our minds and hearts focused on the things of the Lord. We must walk by faith and not by sight (2 Cor. 5:7).

Our hearts become hardened when we spend time thinking about anything other than God and His ways. In this case, the disciples weren't thinking about things like murder, adultery, or theft. Their thinking was totally occupied with the storm and how they could save their lives. However, they were considering only natural ways of deliverance. They should have been considering a miraculous deliverance since they were in obedience to Jesus' command.

Mark 6:52 links their hardness of heart to them not considering the miracle of the feeding of the five thousand. If they had kept their thinking on the miracle they had just seen, then they wouldn't have been amazed to see Jesus walking on the water toward them. After all, He had compelled them to get into the ship (Mark 6:45 and Matt. 14:22) and was responsible for them.

He was also just a short distance away from them and in the same storm. So, they knew He was aware of their situation. They should have been expecting Jesus to come and save them, even if He had to walk on the water to do it. Certainly, a man who could feed thousands of people with five loaves and two fishes and have more left over when He finished than when He started, could walk on water too.

OVERCOME YOUR RESISTANCE

And straightway [Jesus] constrained his disciples to get into the ship, and to go to the other side before unto Bethsaida, while he sent away the people.

Mark 6:45

The *Modern English Version* translation of this verse says that Jesus "compelled" the disciples. Using "compelled" or "constrained" means that there was a resistance on their part. They didn't want to get into the boat.

If you read on in the chapter, you'll learn that a storm was brewing. A number of these disciples—Peter, Andrew, James, and John—had likely been in this situation before. They were raised on that lake. They were fishermen. This is how they made their living.

The disciples could tell that the conditions weren't good and knew it was dangerous to be out on the Sea of Galilee in a storm at night. So, there was resistance on their part. And yet, Jesus compelled them to get into the ship.

The disciples were doing this against their better judgment, but in obedience to Jesus, they went out in that ship and headed toward the other side. They put the boat and their lives at risk just because of their commitment to Jesus.

Years ago, I took a boat trip across the Sea of Galilee. Under normal circumstances, it would probably take two hours or less to cross that body of water. The disciples entered their boat at about sunset, and by the middle of the night, they were only halfway across. So, the disciples had already been in that boat about nine hours because "*the wind was contrary unto them*" (Mark 6:48).

If these disciples really wanted to, they could have turned that boat around and headed back to where they had come from. And since they were experienced on that lake and would've had a strong wind behind them, they may have made it back to shore in a relatively short time. But because of their love and obedience to the Lord, they were still headed in the direction that the Lord gave them.

Hardness of heart can happen to people who love God and seek after Him. Today, we live in a culture that promotes many things contrary to the principles of God. People are flaunting things like homosexuality when the Bible absolutely condemns it as being an abomination to God.

If a person isn't maintaining a personal, living relationship with God, they can become desensitized. As Jesus warned in Matthew 24:12, *"because iniquity shall abound, the love of many shall wax cold."* Their hearts will be hardened, and they won't persist in what the Lord called them to do.

It's been said that if you put a frog into a pot of boiling water, it will instantly jump out. But if you put it in room temperature water and just gradually turn up the heat, it'll stay in there until it boils to death, because it came on gradually. I believe something similar has happened to many Christians today. As a society, we have become desensitized to all kinds of ungodliness and perversion, and it has affected our hearts. It has affected the way we relate to God—and we don't even know it.

'DON"T YOU CARE?'

And the same day, when the even was come, he saith unto them, Let us pass over unto the other side. And when they had sent away the multitude, they took him even as he was in the ship. And there were also with him other little ships. And there arose a great storm of wind, and the waves beat into the ship, so that it was now full. And he was in the hinder part of the ship, asleep on a pillow: and they awake him, and say unto him, Master, carest thou not that we perish?

Mark 4:35–38

In this instance, Jesus called the disciples to take Him across the Sea of Galilee after a day when He had just taught thirteen parables. He had revealed to the disciples all of these great truths about how the kingdom of God works by the seed of His word the same way this natural world is dependent on physical seeds. And yet, in the middle of a storm, just a few hours later, they asked Him, "Don't you care that we're perishing?"

Today, it's easy for us to condemn them and think, *How dare they say something like that to Jesus?* But how many times have Christians said something similar to the Lord? People cry out to God and say things like, "I'm dying," "I've got this pain," "My marriage is falling apart," "My business is failing." They call it prayer, but what they're actually saying is, "God, You don't seem to care. Why won't You do something?"

Charles Capps was a minister in the twentieth century who taught on the believer's authority in Christ and the power of faith-filled words. Years ago, he was troubled about something and said, "Father, I prayed, but it's not working out." And the Lord stopped him and asked, "What are you doing?" Charles responded, "I'm praying." But the Lord corrected him by saying, "No, you're not. You're complaining!"[3]

That's exactly what these disciples were doing. They were in an open boat that was full of water, so Jesus knew what was going on. This was a serious situation! He knew that they were struggling, but He was sound asleep on a pillow. In the disciples' eyes, Jesus didn't appear to care about their situation.

Jesus didn't say, "Guys, I'm sorry. I know you're just human. I'm the Son of God, so I should've done something." Instead, He rose up, rebuked the wind, stilled the waters with His word, and turned to the disciples to ask, "*Why are ye so fearful? how is it that ye have no faith?*" (Mark 4:39–40). Remember, Jesus had just taught them how the kingdom of God works. He had given them a word to go to the other side. That was His part. In a sense, this was an opportunity to put those things into practice by acting on the word He had given them. That was their part.

INCLINE YOUR EAR

My son, attend to my words; incline thine ear unto my sayings. Let them not depart from thine eyes; keep them in the midst of thine heart. For they are *life unto those that find them, and health to all their flesh.*

Proverbs 4:20–22

I was meditating on this passage once and asked, "God, what does '*incline thine ear*' mean?" The Lord showed me that He wasn't talking about the way you hold your head. He was talking about how to pay attention.

The Hebrew word used for "attend" in that verse literally means, "to prick up the ears; harken."[2] This describes the way a horse or mule rotates their ears to amplify sounds. They are focusing their attention on the noise and where it is coming from. Like them, we need to direct our attention to God's word, and it will sensitize our hearts towards Him.

When I was in Vietnam, I was stationed on a fire support base. There were always bombs going off, rockets being fired, and mortars blasting away. Often, we'd take ten to fifteen direct hits a day, with one or two of them landing right on top of my bunker. It withstood the blasts, but there would be a cloud of dust, and everything would be knocked off the shelf. Finally, I just got used to everything. I just tuned it all out.

One day, I pulled guard duty in a bunker that was about a hundred yards down the hill, so it was more exposed to enemy fire. There were four of us on duty. I had the first watch. Two of the guys went below to sleep, and the other guy, a Puerto Rican, stayed on top with me. He was a draftee, and the only thing he said in English was, "forty days," no matter what you asked him. He took the second watch, and I went to sleep right next to him on top of that bunker.

At about 5 a.m., I woke up, and that Puerto Rican guy wasn't there. I looked below, and the other two guys weren't there either. We were supposed to stay on guard duty until 6 a.m., so I stayed for that final hour and then went back up the hill. Suddenly, the chaplain ran up to me and asked, "Are you alright?" I had no idea what they were talking about.

It turned out that something went wrong with that Puerto Rican guy in the middle of the night, and he started firing weapons everywhere. He shot over five hundred M16 rounds, tossed over one hundred hand grenades, used the grenade launcher about one hundred times, and detonated every Claymore mine.

The two guys below got scared and ran off. The others up the hill were going to blow away the Puerto Rican, but they held their fire because I was still there. Finally, he ran out of ammunition, and they captured him. And I slept through the whole thing!

You see, I was so used to explosions that they no longer disturbed my sleep; they didn't even register. But when I was in my bunker, the slightest creak of a hinge on my bunker door would wake me up. I had inclined my ears to be sensitive to certain things while ignoring others.

Every one of us does this. Some live in the flight path of a noisy airport or on busy city streets. They might live next to a train track and get used to those sounds. But let their baby breathe hard or make the slightest sound like they are sick, and they bolt wide awake. That's being sensitive to baby noises while being hardened to these other sounds.

The same thing happens in the supernatural. You can be sensitive to what you want and be hardened to everything else.

DO YOU REMEMBER?

Having eyes, see ye not? and having ears, hear ye not? and do ye not remember?

Mark 8:18

A condition of a hardened heart is insensitivity to hearing the voice of God. I've heard people say, "You talk like God speaks to you all of the time. But the devil told me I'm never going to hear the voice of God."

Jesus said, "*My sheep hear my voice*" (John 10:27), and the voice of "*a stranger will they not follow*" (John 10:5). But for most people, it's exactly the opposite of what Jesus said. People hear the slightest whisper of unbelief, anger, unforgiveness, or bitterness, and they'll respond to that. But then they say, "I just can't hear the voice of God." Something's wrong with this picture!

Whatever you focus on, you are going to be sensitive to. Perhaps you're struggling to hear the voice of God, but you easily hear and respond to the voice of doubt or fear. Maybe you know all the sports statistics or the words to your favorite movie or song, but you can't seem to remember a scripture to stand on in a crisis. If these things describe your condition, then you've got a sensitive heart to those things you are focused on, but a hardened heart to the things of God you've neglected.

Now, you may have surface-level knowledge of things, but if you don't focus on them, you will become hardened toward them. It's like that in school. The night before a test, you could cram all the necessary information into your short-term memory just to pass. But unless you continue to focus on those things, you won't retain them. Someone could come up to you months later and ask you the same questions that were on your exam—and you'd fail!

FIX YOUR RECEIVER

Be still, and know that I am God: I will be exalted among the heathen, I will be exalted in the earth.

Psalm 46:10

Did you know there are radio and TV signals all around you? The stations in your area are likely broadcasting twenty-four hours a day, seven days a week. But many people don't hear those broadcasts because they don't have a receiver.

I remember being a kid, listening to the radio. The radio signal would fluctuate. You had to constantly adjust the dial to keep the station coming in clearly. For TVs, we used "rabbit-ear" antennas on top of the TV and often had to stand and hold them to improve reception. Today's receivers are much better. They have built-in technology that constantly adjusts to the selected frequency and keeps the signal constant.

We didn't have the internet or satellite radio like they do today, where you could listen to stations from just about anywhere in the world. You had to be within range of a transmitter if you wanted to listen to music or programs.

If a person was listening in their car, and they drove away from the station they were listening to, the signal would get weaker, causing a static sound to mix with the music. As long as they were still within range of the transmitter, they could manually adjust—or tune—the dial to better hear that station. The broadcasters weren't adjusting their signals to accommodate people. It was up to the listener to tune their receiver to a station and receive the signal.

The same is true with God. The Lord is constantly speaking, but few people are tuned in and listening. Most Christians are just pleading with God in prayer to transmit when the problem is that they are the ones not receiving.

If this sounds like you, the first thing you need to do is fix your receiver. You need to believe that God is already speaking to you and then start listening. But that takes time, effort, and focus. The average Christian's lifestyle is so busy, it isn't conducive to hearing God's voice.

For example, what is your typical answer to the question, "How are you?" Many of you probably answer something about being very busy. I often say, "I'm busier than a one-armed paper hanger!" And, to a degree, that's true.

Once, the Lord revealed some things to me about Psalm 46:10. To get a better understanding of what He meant, I spent a whole afternoon just sitting outside and being perfectly still. I had chipmunks crawl up my legs because I was so still. I saw thousands of ants. I could hear the wind blowing through the trees and making noise. I could even hear crows flapping their wings as they flew by. These things were happening all around me, but I usually didn't notice them.

The Lord showed me that it's in stillness, not busyness, that we tune our spiritual ears to hear Him. The Lord always speaks to us in that *still small voice* (1 Kgs. 19:12), but often it's drowned out amid all the static of our daily lives.

PHARAOH'S EXAMPLE

And I will harden Pharaoh's heart, and multiply my signs and my wonders in the land of Egypt. But Pharaoh shall not hearken unto you, that I may lay my hand upon Egypt, and bring forth mine armies, and *my people the children of Israel, out of the land of Egypt by great judgments.*

Exodus 7:3–4

Pharaoh is the supreme example of hard-heartedness. He hardened his heart against the Lord by proclaiming himself to be a god. That was his choice, and the Lord enforced his decision by hardening his heart even more. When God hardens your heart, you're in trouble. Pharaoh saw the miracles of God and experienced all the plagues on Egypt, but after each one, he'd be hardened and persist in his ways.

For example, when the plague of the frogs came (Ex. 8:1–6), they were everywhere—frogs were in their shoes, in their food, in their clothes, and over the entire land. Finally, Pharaoh called Moses and said, "*Intreat the Lord, that he may take away the frogs from me, and from my people*" (Ex. 8:8). Seemingly, Pharaoh had come to his senses, humbled himself, and admitted that it was God who was doing all this.

But when Moses asked when he should remove the plague, Pharaoh said, "Tomorrow" (Ex. 8:10). That's what hardness of heart can do. Pharaoh was humbled, destroyed, and brought to his knees. He could have asked for the frogs to leave instantly. But Pharaoh said, "Tomorrow." That's a hard heart. And once he saw the plague ended, his heart was hardened against Moses and Israel even more—and more plagues came.

After his firstborn was killed, Pharaoh finally let the children of Israel go (Ex. 12:29–32). Pharaoh had been defeated, and he acknowledged it. Then, the Bible says that God hardened Pharaoh's heart again (Ex. 14:4). Immediately, he lost all of his perception, wisdom, and good sense, and went after the children of Israel. It would be impossible for anybody to be that irrational without help!

The children of Israel were camped in a valley—with the mountains on two sides and the Red Sea at the end. Pharaoh and his armies came upon them and saw them trapped there. When the children of Israel left Egypt, a pillar of cloud by day and fire by night went in front of them to guide them (Ex. 13:21–22). But when they prepared to cross the Red Sea, the pillar moved behind them, settling between them and the Egyptians (Ex. 14:19).

Now, if you're hard-hearted enough to chase the Israelites after the Lord had humiliated you like that, it seems you'd wise up when the supernatural fire of God appeared. But Pharaoh and the Egyptians just stayed there, looking at that pillar of fire and cloud all night while the Israelites crossed the Red Sea. *Then* they started after them. It wasn't until the Lord took off their chariot wheels that one of their lightning-fast minds said, "The Lord fights for the Israelites" (Ex. 14:25). That's what a hardened heart will do to you. It makes you stupid. But it was too late—the sea collapsed and destroyed the Egyptians completely!

I believe that a hardened heart limits your ability to think and function spiritually. But under the New Covenant, God does not harden our hearts. It's we who allow our hearts to be hardened against God.

YOU HAVE CONTROL

Take heed, brethren, lest there be in any of you an evil heart of unbelief, in departing from the living God. But exhort one another daily, while it is called To day; lest any of you be hardened through the deceitfulness of sin.

Hebrews 3:12–13

You are the one who has control over whether your heart is sensitive to God, or if it's cold, insensitive, unfeeling, or unyielding—in other words, hardened. If that's your condition, you could pray, *God, please change my heart!* But ultimately, you are in control of it, and there are things you must do to make your heart more sensitive.

First, if you're living in sin, stop it! Because it's only going to harden your heart (Heb. 3:13). You cannot live in sin and have a heart sensitive towards God. Also, Hebrews 12:1 says, "*let us lay aside every weight, and the sin which doth so easily beset* us." You can be encumbered by things that weigh you down.

Just as a runner has to remove weights to achieve the best results, we need to rid ourselves of things that keep us from getting maximum results. These weights can differ from person to person, but things that occupy our time and distract us from God are certainly weights in our spiritual race (Mark 4:19).

Whatever you focus your attention on is what will dominate you. Proverbs 23:7 says that whatever a man thinks "*in his heart, so* is *he*." Conversely, whatever you don't focus on cannot dominate you.

The Bible says the disciples' hearts were hardened because they did not consider—focus on, or think about—the miracle of the loaves. They disregarded what God had done in their presence and didn't give it priority. On the other hand, if they had meditated totally on what Jesus did—feeding five thousand people with five loaves and two fish—that would have ministered faith to them. This reveals that whatever we consider we become sensitive to, and whatever we neglect, we become hardened to. The vast majority of the church today has become hardened to the things of God, not through sin but neglect and preoccupation with the things of this world.

For example, maybe the average Christian truly loves God, but if they were honest, they may say they're not fully confident in their ability to receive or minister healing. If someone near them were dying right now, they may call on their pastor or some other "man of faith" to pray. But if they were asked to pray, they wouldn't be confident in their own ability.

But you don't have to be a prophet or apostle to have God's power work through you. You just have to believe. The Lord said that believers would lay hands on the sick and see them recover (Mark 16:18). Jesus said that believers would do the same works He did (John 14:12). If you aren't confident doing those same works, it's because you relate to the natural more than the supernatural. That's a hardened heart.

Again, it comes back to what you are focusing your attention on. You may not be living in rebellion and sin. But you may have simply neglected meditating on the things of God in your life. Now, I'm not condemning anyone. But to see things change, we have to start considering the things of God.

'NO WICKED THING'

I will set no wicked thing before mine eyes: I hate the work of them that turn aside; it shall not cleave to me.

Psalm 101:3

Not long after I got really turned on to the Lord on March 23, 1968, my mother took me on a trip to Bern, Switzerland, for a Baptist youth conference with Billy Graham. Along the way, we stopped in New York City. We were staying in a hotel in Times Square, and I had never seen anything like what was going on around me—my jaw just dropped! But I had hundreds of Gospel tracts, and I was excited about handing them out and witnessing for the Lord.

At about 2 a.m., I was walking down the alleys in the city. When I saw a group of people, I'd go up to them, pass out tracts, and tell them about the Lord. That may not have been smart, but because I was following God and not filling myself with the sewage of the world, I didn't even know enough to be afraid. I hadn't heard about gangs and therefore had zero fear. I shared the Gospel with these people who were probably up to no good, and I just cleared out all the alleys in the wee hours of the morning.

There must have been a hundred prostitutes lined up along a wall, but I wasn't sharp enough to realize what they were doing. I just thought, *This is awesome! Here are all these women I can witness to!* So, I went down the row, gave each of them a tract, started preaching, and I cleaned out the entire street. They all left!

At some point, a pimp came up to me and tried to sell me one of his girls. He was using all this street language, but I just couldn't understand him. Because I was so naive, it just didn't register. After a few minutes, this pimp just threw up his hands, shook his head, and walked off! He must have been thinking, *What rock did this guy crawl out from under?*

When I got back to the hotel room, I started explaining what happened to the guys I was staying with. I said, "You will never believe what this guy was saying to me!" And I started telling them what that pimp said. They started laughing and told me he was trying to offer one of his prostitutes. Thank God I didn't know what he had been talking about. I was so focused on God and wanted to serve Him that I was hardened to what the devil was offering me. Instead, I ended up witnessing to everyone on the street about Jesus.

Through that whole experience, I didn't know enough to be tempted because I didn't think on things like that, so I wasn't the least bit tempted. It didn't dawn on me that people did those things. I didn't have to pray, "Oh Jesus, help me to resist!" I didn't have to resist anything. I was hardened to those temptations through neglect.

YOU CAN'T BE TEMPTED WITH WHAT YOU DON'T THINK

And truly, if they had been mindful of that country *from whence they came out, they might have had opportunity to have returned.*

Hebrews 11:15

This is one of the most powerful scriptures in the Word of God.

The Lord had commanded Abraham and Sarah to leave Ur of the Chaldees and dwell in the land of Canaan. Going back to Ur would have been sin for them. This verse says that if they had thought about returning to Ur, they would have been tempted to do it. But since they didn't even consider it, that means they weren't even tempted. Wow! You and I could be awesome men and women of God if we were never tempted to do anything else.

And that's the key to this verse. You can't be tempted with something you have never thought of. Therefore, if we keep our minds stayed on the Lord and don't think on ungodly or carnal things, we won't even be tempted to sin or fail. All we will be able to relate to is victory and abundant life. Amen!

KNOW YOUR BUSINESS

I saw two people raised from the dead in the early years of my ministry. That got me so fired up that I thought if I could experience people coming back from death, then I could see any miracle. At the next meeting I conducted, there was a man in a wheelchair sitting in the front row. I could hardly wait to get through preaching so I could pray for him.

I jumped off the stage, grabbed him by the hand, and pulled him out of his wheelchair. He fell right on his face since he was a quadriplegic and couldn't catch himself. There was a loud gasp from the crowd, and fear hit me. I was thinking that a lawsuit or at least a lot of criticism was about to come my way.

I hugged him and put him back in his chair and said, "*Depart in peace, be ye warmed and filled...*" (James 2:16), but I didn't give him what he needed—healing. That really bothered me. I knew I had faith. I had seen the dead raised, and I was totally expecting this man to get up and walk. Otherwise, I would never have pulled him out of his wheelchair.

I went to my room that night, totally confused. For at least two years, I sought the Lord for an answer about what went wrong. Then I finally came across a story about Smith Wigglesworth in a book written by his son-in-law.

Back in the early twentieth century, all kinds of miracles manifested through Smith Wigglesworth's ministry. He is considered a forerunner of the great Healing Revival of the 1940s and 50s and is still widely revered by Christians today.

One of the criticisms spoken against Smith Wigglesworth was that he was cold, insensitive, unfeeling, and unyielding (or hardened). Indeed, he *was* cold, insensitive, unfeeling, and unyielding—*to anything but God!* He did not pity people with disease and sickness. That sounds extreme, but in over forty years of ministry, he never laid his hands on a person who wasn't healed.

In his meetings, Smith would often say, "The first person to stand up will be healed of whatever problem he has." In one meeting, a woman who had a huge tumor on her belly stood. It looked like she was nine months pregnant. Two other ladies stood with her, holding her up.

She was in terrible pain, and her legs were so thin she could not stand by herself. They helped the woman on the platform, and Smith said, "Let her go." The two ladies with her answered, "She can't stand if we let her go—she'll fall." So, he said again, "Let her go." They let her go, and she fell over with a thud.

You could imagine what the crowd thought. Smith said, "Pick her up." So, they picked her up, and again he said, "Let her go." They said, "We can't let her go, she'll fall," so he raised his voice and said, "Let her go!" They let her go, and she fell again, crying out in pain. So, they picked her up. For the third time, Smith said, "Let her go." They answered, "We will not let her go—that's cruel!" So, he raised his voice again and said, "Let her go!" They answered, "No!"

Just then, a man stood up in the audience and yelled, "You callous brute—leave her alone!" But Smith yelled back, "You mind your own business. I know mine." Smith yelled again and said, "Let her go!" They let her go, and that tumor just fell on the floor. That woman walked right out of there healed!

Do you know why it worked for him? Because he was sensitive to God and hardened to anything that looked contrary. He was hardened to his senses, even his good, natural senses, so that he was not moved by anything except what God had told him. That's why it worked.

The Lord revealed to me that Smith didn't have any more faith than I did, but he had a lot less unbelief. He didn't see the positive results with this lady the first or second time. That was just like me with this man in the wheelchair. But the difference was that he wasn't moved by what he saw or what the people thought. I was. I got into unbelief because I was more sensitive to the negative than I was the promise of God's Word that when I laid hands on the sick, they would recover (Mark 16:18).

People like Smith Wigglesworth see great miracles in their lives because they live a "separated life." But some people have misinterpreted what that means. They say it means if you have any sin in your life, God won't use you, but if you're totally pure, He will.

That's foolish because you can never be good enough. It's not a person's holiness that earns them anything from God. But their separation sensitizes them to what they already have from God. If they focus all of their attention on that, they won't allow temptation to enter.

STAY SENSITIVE

A man named Sadu Sundar Singh was a legend in India in the early 1900s. If you mention his name there, people begin talking about all the miracles that happened. He was a Muslim who converted to Christ, and many people were healed through his ministry.

In Bombay (Mumbai), for example, he saw as many as one hundred thousand people healed in a single day. He would go into a city and empty all the morgues, raising dozens of people from the dead. It was phenomenal! Singh finally had to stop praying for people because nobody would listen to him preach— they just thronged him to get at the healing power of God.

Singh saw tremendous things happen in India, but in the United States, it was a totally different story. I've heard a story that he once planned a lengthy tour of America. After traveling by ship, he got off the boat in New York City and spent thirty minutes walking around the city. Then, he promptly canceled his speaking engagements and got back on the boat.

Sadu Sundar Singh said, "I'll never preach to these people. They're so hard-hearted and so busy, they'll never hear it." And he went back to India. He knew that where people are preoccupied with other things, the Gospel will never penetrate. And that was over a hundred years ago!

For years, we didn't watch television in our home. It wasn't because we were trying to be particularly holy or anything. It was just that I wanted to keep my heart sensitive to God, so I could hear His voice clearly.

Again, I'm not condemning anyone. My wife and I will watch television these days, but when commercials promoting sickness or other ungodly things come on, we press the mute button until they're over. I don't want to be thinking about the side effects caused by some medicine; I want my mind focused on the healing power of God.

Back during the COVID pandemic in 2020, I called all my employees together to update them on our response, and to encourage them that they didn't need to receive sickness. I was standing on Psalm 91 and believing that no plague would come near my dwelling (Ps. 91:10)—my body! I didn't turn on the news and listen to all the doubt and fear going on at that time. And because of that, I stayed well when other people got sick.

Now, there were ministers who criticized me for taking a stand. They said, "Who does he think he is? You just can't live that way." Well, they're too late to change my mind because this is how I'm living!

I've stayed focused on the things of God all these years, and our ministry has seen people healed, blind eyes opened, and people raised from the dead. And I believe it's because I've kept my heart sensitive to God and hardened to the things of the world!

DON'T ENTERTAIN SIN

But every man is tempted, when he is drawn away of his own lust, and enticed. Then when lust hath conceived, it bringeth forth sin: and sin, when it is finished, bringeth forth death.

James 1:14–15

Some people think yielding to temptation is inevitable, that a certain part of a person is just bent on sinning. That may be true of people who are not born again and still have an old sin nature on the inside of them. But there is nothing within a Christian that makes them sin.

It is the nature of a born-again person to operate in the fruit of the Spirit—love, joy, peace, longsuffering, gentleness, goodness, faith, meekness, and temperance (Gal. 5:22–23). That is normal. That means the reason why contrary thoughts take root in our minds is because we entertain them—we consider them.

You see, sin has to be conceived (James 1:15), just as a child has to be conceived. If you stop the conception by refusing to meditate on sinful things, then you don't have to fight such a strong battle when temptation presents itself. But many

Christians wait until a battle is raging in their minds, and only then do they try to summon up faith, rebuke the devil, use the name of Jesus, and overcome temptation. There is a better way—stop the temptation before it starts!

When I served in Vietnam, I lived surrounded by doubt and unbelief twenty-four hours a day. I saw myself victorious over sin in every situation—but not without effort. This was after the Lord touched my life on March 23, 1968, but still a few years before I started praying in tongues. So, I didn't know all the things that I know now. Years later, I read the letters I sent home to my mother, and they were just pitiful. I was very sin conscious—but I was still determined to serve God and honor Him.

There were opportunities to sin all around me. For example, one transient bunker I stayed in had the walls and ceilings plastered with pictures of nude women. So, the only way to avoid those things was to literally stick my nose in the Bible all the waking hours I was in there.

The thing I hated most was the ungodly language. I was determined not to hear that stuff, so I got a poster board and wrote, "*Thou shalt not take the name of the Lord thy God in vain*" (Ex. 20:7) in big letters and hung it on the wall. That stopped all the profanity in my bunker. In fact, they stopped talking to me altogether, but that was still better than having to hear all their profanity and perversion.

If you neglect the things of God, you will be hardened toward Him. But if you neglect the devil, you will find that you'll become hardened (cold, insensitive, unfeeling, and unyielding) towards the devil. It's just that simple.

DEAL WITH UNBELIEF

And Jesus said unto them, Because of your unbelief: for verily I say unto you, If ye have faith as a grain of mustard seed, ye shall say unto this mountain, Remove hence to yonder place; and it shall remove; and nothing shall be impossible unto you.

Matthew 17:20

When a man brought his son, who was "*lunatick, and sore vexed*" (Matt. 17:15) to Jesus' disciples to "*cure him*" (Matt. 17:16), Jesus used it as an opportunity to teach about belief and unbelief. The disciples couldn't get the job done, but Jesus cast the devil out of the boy, and he "*was cured from that very hour*" (Matt. 17:18). Afterward, the disciples came to Jesus and asked, "Why couldn't we do it?" (Matt. 17:19).

If it's God's will to heal, and Jesus healed this boy, why didn't the disciples get him healed? They believed that it was God's will to heal. They knew they had the power to cast these demons out. They had already been given authority to heal the sick and cast out devils (Matt. 10:1 and 8).

If we look at Mark's account of this same story, when the father saw his son having a seizure (Mark 9:20–22), he looked at Jesus and said, "If you can do anything, help us." He began to doubt and despair. He was looking at the situation and saying, "God, I don't know if You can even handle this." But Jesus said, "If you can believe, all things are possible to him that believes" (Mark 9:23).

The man's response to Jesus is very telling: "*Lord, I believe; help thou mine unbelief*" (Mark 9:24). Notice the Lord didn't correct him. Jesus just turned around and cured the boy. This shows that you can have faith and yet have unbelief at the same time.

Belief is like a team of horses hooked up to a wagon. Under normal circumstances, they would have enough power and be able to move that wagon easily. But if you hooked an equal team of horses up to the other side of the wagon and had them pull simultaneously in the opposite direction, the net effect would be zero. Both teams would be pulling on that wagon with all their strength, and it wouldn't move because they're canceling each other out. That is what happens with unbelief.

Another example of this would be a balloon filled with helium. Normally, it would rise, but if it has weights attached to it, it will stay earthbound, even though it has the potential to float. The weights are a force that negates its potential to rise.

This is what Jesus was saying in Matthew 17:20. He didn't tell His disciples, "It's because you don't have enough faith." He said, "It's because of your unbelief. Your unbelief canceled out the faith you had." Also, notice that Jesus said, "*this kind goeth not out but by prayer and fasting*" (Matt. 17:21).

It's traditionally taught that Jesus was referring to the demon who was afflicting this boy. But, if you look at the context of what Jesus was teaching, He was saying that fasting and prayer are the only ways of casting out this type of unbelief.

The type of unbelief in this situation came from their natural senses. The demon convulsed the boy and what they saw was contrary to what they were believing for. So, faith was present, but the unbelief that came from what they saw negated their faith. It was a weight that kept their faith from rising and producing the results they wanted. The only way to overcome that natural type of unbelief is to spend time, quality and quantity time, in the presence of the Lord through prayer and fasting.

That was the problem with me and the man I pulled out of the wheelchair. I did have faith, but unbelief—my fear of what he and the people in the crowd thought—cancelled out my faith. My heart was sensitive to men and, therefore, hardened towards God.

HAVE CONFIDENCE IN THE WORD

I remember the first person I ever saw healed. I was teaching a Baptist Sunday School class, and I hadn't yet gotten the revelation that healing is God's will for everyone. You see, our church chose to preach forgiveness of sins as all there was to salvation.

They didn't teach on healing the way our ministry does now. I praise God for all the people who were born again in that church, and that they taught me how to value the Word, but they focused on those things at the expense of healing.

They believed that God *could* heal, but they didn't believe it was His will to heal every time. They certainly didn't understand that they had any authority over healing. The best they would do was just pray and say, "God, if it be Your will."

But then I saw in the Bible that believers *"shall lay hands on the sick, and they shall recover"* (Mark 16:18). I began reading that verse to my class—a group of high school students—every Sunday. I had read that verse and similar ones many times over the years, but once I got turned on to the Lord and became sensitive to the things of God, the Holy Spirit just made the Bible come alive to me.

I told my class, "I know this isn't what the Baptists teach, and I've never personally seen it, but it's in God's Word, so we're going to lay hands on the sick and they will recover. If you get sick, don't stay away from church. We'll lay hands on you."

Not long after that, a girl came in sick. She was so sick she actually looked green! When I saw her, my first reaction was, "What are you doing here?" Then she said, "Well, you said if I was sick, I should come and have you lay hands on me." I had already forgotten what I told the class! So, we sat her down in a chair and prayed, but by the time we were done, she looked worse than before. Finally, she started feeling so sick that she had to go home.

Later, I went into the church service feeling really defeated. I thought, *God, I did exactly what You said in Your Word to the best of my ability. Why didn't it work?* At this point, I had the opportunity to give in to unbelief. But during the song service, I looked around and saw that girl in the back of the church, frantically waving at me. When I went back there, she said, "By the time I got home, I was totally healed!"

Now, I've grown a lot since then. And because I put confidence in the Word of God and keep my heart sensitive to the Lord, I've seen countless miracles. I've become hardened to doubt, fear, and unbelief while remaining sensitive to all the good things God has provided through Jesus Christ.

CONCLUSION

What I've shared is not some "great revelation," but it is practical. It will work. And if you implement these things in your life, you are on your way to succeeding.

If you make the Word of God a priority and just do what it says, you will see results. It's simple—but it's not easy. You have to choose what you will set your mind on. You decide what to harden your heart to, and what it will be sensitive to.

Putting God first may cost you. It may cost you some of your time, some of your conveniences, and some of your pleasures. It has certainly cost me a lot. I've lost lots of fear, depression, sickness, poverty, and a host of other things I don't miss.

I believe it's worth it. It's worth turning off your television. I may not know all the sports scores or all the surveys and statistics used in creating government policy. I don't even know all the correct terms to use when discussing those things. But I haven't missed a thing by not knowing. I tell people, "If it isn't in the Bible, I don't know it." And in my life, that has made a huge difference!

There is nothing hard about the Gospel. It doesn't take great talent. All it takes is a great commitment, and it will change your life.

FURTHER STUDY

If you enjoyed this booklet and would like to learn more about some of the things I've shared, I suggest my teachings:

1. *Effortless Change*
2. *You Are Plain as Dirt*
3. *The Heart of Man*
4. *Discover the Keys to Staying Full of God*
5. *Are You Satisfied with Jesus?*

Plus 200,000 hours of free teaching on our website.

These teachings are available for free at **awmi.net**, or they can be purchased at **awmi.net/store**.

Go deeper in your relationship with God by browsing all of Andrew's free teachings.

RECEIVE JESUS AS
YOUR SAVIOR

Choosing to receive Jesus Christ as your Lord and Savior is the most important decision you'll ever make!

God's Word promises, *"That if thou shalt confess with thy mouth the Lord Jesus, and shalt believe in thine heart that God hath raised him from the dead, thou shalt be saved. For with the heart man believeth unto righteousness; and with the mouth confession is made unto salvation"* (Rom. 10:9–10). *"For whosoever shall call upon the name of the Lord shall be saved"* (Rom. 10:13). By His grace, God has already done everything to provide salvation. Your part is simply to believe and receive.

Pray out loud: "Jesus, I acknowledge that I've sinned and need to receive what you did for the forgiveness of my sins. I confess that You are my Lord and Savior. I believe in my heart that God raised You from the dead. By faith in Your Word, I receive salvation now. Thank You for saving me."

The very moment you commit your life to Jesus Christ, the truth of His Word instantly comes to pass in your spirit. Now that you're born again, there's a brand-new you!

Please contact us and let us know that you've prayed to receive Jesus as your Savior. We'd like to send you some free materials to help you on your new journey. Call our Helpline:

719-635-1111 (available 24 hours a day, seven days a week) to speak to a staff member who is here to help you understand and grow in your new relationship with the Lord.

Welcome to your new life!

RECEIVE THE HOLY SPIRIT

As His child, your loving heavenly Father wants to give you the supernatural power you need to live a new life. *"For every one that asketh receiveth; and he that seeketh findeth; and to him that knocketh it shall be opened...how much more shall* your *heavenly Father give the Holy Spirit to them that ask him?"* (Luke 11:10–13).

All you have to do is ask, believe, and receive! Pray this: "Father, I recognize my need for Your power to live a new life. Please fill me with Your Holy Spirit. By faith, I receive it right now. Thank You for baptizing me. Holy Spirit, You are welcome in my life."

Some syllables from a language you don't recognize will rise up from your heart to your mouth (1 Cor. 14:14). As you speak them out loud by faith, you're releasing God's power from within and building yourself up in the spirit (1 Cor. 14:4). You can do this whenever and wherever you like.

It doesn't really matter whether you felt anything or not when you prayed to receive the Lord and His Spirit. If you believed in your heart that you received, then God's Word promises you did.

"Therefore I say unto you, What things soever ye desire, when ye pray, believe that ye receive them, and ye shall have them" (Mark 11:24). God always honors His Word—believe it!

We would like to rejoice with you, pray with you, and answer any questions to help you understand more fully what has taken place in your life!

Please contact us to let us know that you've prayed to be filled with the Holy Spirit and to request the book *The New You & the Holy Spirit*. This book will explain in more detail about the benefits of being filled with the Holy Spirit and speaking in tongues. Call our Helpline: **719-635-1111** (available 24 hours a day, seven days a week).

ENDNOTES

1. Webster's Dictionary 1828, s.v. "consider," Accessed September 3, 2025, https://webstersdictionary1828.com/Dictionary/consider

2. Strong's Definitions, s.v. "qâshab" ("בָשַׁק"), accessed September 3, 2025, https://www.blueletterbible.org/lexicon/h7181/kjv/wlc/0-1/ ca

3. Charles Capps, "Decrees: Their Force & Power," Harrison House, Accessed January 16, 2025, https://harrisonhouse.com/blog/charles-capps-decrees-their-force-and-power

CALL FOR PRAYER

If you need prayer for any reason, you can call our Helpline, 24 hours a day, seven days a week at **719-635-1111**. A trained prayer minister will answer your call and pray with you.

Every day, we receive testimonies of healings and other miracles from our Helpline, and we are ministering God's nearly-too-good-to-be-true message of the Gospel to more people than ever. So, I encourage you to call today!

ABOUT THE AUTHOR

Andrew Wommack's life was forever changed the moment he encountered the supernatural love of God on March 23, 1968. As a renowned Bible teacher and author, Andrew has made it his mission to change the way the world sees God.

Andrew's vision is to go as far and deep with the Gospel as possible. His message goes far through the *Gospel Truth* television program, which is available to over half the world's population. The message goes deep through discipleship at Charis Bible College, headquartered in Woodland Park, Colorado. Founded in 1994, Charis has campuses across the United States and around the globe.

Andrew also has an extensive library of teaching materials in print, audio, and video. More than 200,000 hours of free teachings can be accessed at **awmi.net**.

CONTACT INFORMATION

Andrew Wommack Ministries, Inc.

PO Box 3333

Colorado Springs, CO 80934-3333

info@awmi.net

awmi.net

Helpline: 719-635-1111 (available 24/7)

Charis Bible College

info@charisbiblecollege.org

844-360-9577

CharisBibleCollege.org

For a complete list of all of our offices,
visit **awmi.net/contact-us**.

Connect with us on social media.

Andrew Wommack's *Living Commentary* digital study Bible is a user-friendly, downloadable program. It's like reading the Bible with Andrew at your side, sharing his revelation with you verse by verse.

Main features:
- Bible study software with a grace-and-faith perspective
- Over 27,000 notes by Andrew on verses from Genesis through Revelation
- *Adam Clarke's Commentary on the Bible*
- *Albert Barnes' Notes on the Whole Bible*
- *Matthew Henry's Concise Commentary*
- 12 Bible versions
- 3 optional premium translation add-ons: *New Living Translation*, *New International Version*, and *The Message* (additional purchase of $9.99 each)
- 2 concordances: *Englishman's Concordance* and *Strong's Concordance*
- 2 dictionaries: *Collaborative International Dictionary* and *Holman's Dictionary*
- Atlas with biblical maps
- Bible and *Living Commentary* statistics
- Quick navigation, including history of verses
- Robust search capabilities (for the Bible and Andrew's notes)
- "Living" (i.e., constantly updated and expanding)
- Ability to create personal notes
- Accessible online and offline

Whether you're new to studying the Bible or a seasoned Bible scholar, you'll gain a deeper revelation of the Word from a grace-and-faith perspective.

Purchase Andrew's *Living Commentary* today at **awmi.net/living** and grow in the Word with Andrew.

Item code: 8350

ANDREW
WOMMACK
MINISTRIES

Sign up to watch anytime, anywhere, for free.

GOSPEL TRUTH
N E T W O R K

There's more on the website!

Discover **FREE** teachings, testimonies, and more by scanning the QR code or visiting **awmi.net**.

Continue to grow in the Word of God!
You will be blessed!

ANDREW WOMMACK MINISTRIES

Your monthly giving makes the greatest kingdom impact.

When you give, you make an impact in the kingdom that lasts for generations. Your generosity enables our phone ministers to answer calls 24/7. Your support is also expanding Charis Bible College and allowing *The Gospel Truth* to reach an even wider global audience. You do this and more through your giving each month!

Become a Grace Partner today! Scan the QR code, visit **awmi.net/partner**, or call our Helpline at **719-635-1111** and select option five for Partnership.

A heart sensitive to the things of God is fully yielded to Him, but many believers find areas where they feel cold or unresponsive. A hardened heart will undermine your faith and weaken your ability to hear and receive from the Lord. When the natural feels more real than the supernatural, and defeat feels more familiar than faith, hardness of heart may be at work. The good news is that God's Word provides the remedy.

In this booklet, learn:

- You have access to supernatural power
- How to become more sensitive to God
- Remembrance can strengthen your faith
- How to identify and remove unbelief

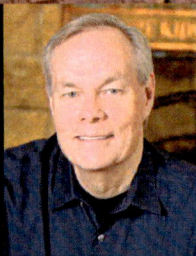

Andrew Wommack

Andrew Wommack, author and Bible teacher, has faithfully served in ministry since answering God's call in 1968. Through his daily *Gospel Truth* broadcasts, he shares the message of Jesus Christ around the world. In 1994, he founded Charis Bible College in Woodland Park, Colorado, which has grown to over 50 campuses globally. Today, he continues to fulfill his mission to take the Gospel as far and as deep as possible through the 24/7 faith-filled programming of the Gospel Truth Network (GTN).

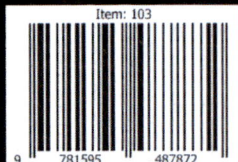

ANDREW WOMMACK MINISTRIES
awmi.net